The Poetical Works of George M. Horton

George Moses Horton

Table of Contents

Table of Contents

The Poetical Works of George M. Horton

George Moses Horton

Kessinger Publishing reprints thousands of hard–to–find books!

Visit us at http://www.kessinger.net

- REGRET FOR THE DEPARTURE OF FRIENDS.
- FAREWELL TO FRANCES.
- THE RETREAT FROM MOSCOW.
- IMPLORING TO BE RESIGNED AT DEATH.
- ON THE PLEASURES OF COLLEGE LIFE.
- THE GRADUATE LEAVING COLLEGE.
- TO THE KING OF MACEDONIA.
- DIVISION OF AN ESTATE.
- PRIDE IN HEAVEN.
- TO MISS TEMPE.
- MAN A TORCH.

The Poetical Works of George M. Horton:
 the colored bard of North Carolina: to which is prefixed the
life of the author, written by himself, by George Moses Horton, 1798? -ca.
1880"

LIFE OF *GEORGE M. HORTON,*

The Colored Bard of North–Carolina.

From the importunate request of a few individuals, I assume the difficult task of writing a concise history of my life. But to open a scene of all the past occurrences of my life I shall not undertake, since I should fail by more than two–thirds in the matter. But if you will condescend to read it, I will endeavor to give a slight specimen entirely clear of exaggeration. A tedious and prolix detail in the matter may not be of any expected, since there is necessarily so much particularity required in a biographical narrative.

I was born in Northampton county, N C., near the line of Virginia, and within four miles of the Roanoke River; the property of William Horton, senior, who also owned my mother, and the whole stock of her children, which were five before me, all girls, but not of one father. I am the oldest child that my mother had by her second husband, and she had four younger than myself, one boy and three girls. But to account for my age is beyond the reach of my power. I was early fond of music, with an extraordinary appetite for singing lively times, for which I was a little remarkable. In the course of a few years after my birth, from the sterility of his land, my old master assumed the notion to move into Chatham, a more fertile and fresh part of country recently settled, and whose waters were far more healthy and agreeable. I here become a cow–boy, which I followed for perhaps ten years in succession, or more. In the course of this disagreeable occupation, I became fond of hearing people read; but being nothing but a poor cow–boy, I had but little or no thought of ever being able to read or spell one word or sentence in any book whatever. My mother discovered my anxiety for books, and strove to encourage my plan; but she, having left her husband behind, was so hard run to make a little shift for herself, that she could give me no assistance in that case. At length I took resolution to learn the alphabet at all events; and lighting by chance at times with some opportunities of being in the presence of school children, I learnt the letters by heart; and fortunately afterwards got hold of some old parts of spelling books abounding with these elements, which I learnt with but little difficulty. And by this time, my brother was deeply excited by the assiduity which he discovered in me, to learn himself; and some of his partial friends strove to put him before me, and I in a stump now, and a sorry instrument to work with at that. But still my brother never could keep time with me. He was indeed an ostentatious youth, and of a far more attractive person than myself, more forward in manly show and early became fond of popularity to an astonishing degree for one of his age and capacity. He strove hard on the wing of ambition to soar above me, and could write a respectable fist before I could form the first letter with a pen, or barely knew the use of a goose–quill. And I must say that he was quite a remarkable youth, as studious as a judge, but much too full of vain lounging among the fair sex.

But to return to the earlier spring of my progress. Though blundering, I became a far better reader than he; but we were indeed both remarkable for boys of color, and hard raising. On well nigh every Sabbath during the year, did I retire away in the summer season to some shady and lonely recess, when I could stammer over the dim and promiscuous syllables in my old black and tattered spelling book, sometimes a piece of one, and then of another; nor would I scarcely spare the time to return to my ordinary meals, being so truly engaged with my book. And by close application to my book at night, my visage became considerably emaciated by extreme perspiration, having no lucubratory aparatus, no candle, no lamp, nor even light–wood, being chiefly raised in oaky woods. Hence I had to sit sweating and smoking over my incompetent bark or brush light, almost exhausted by the heat of the fire, and almost suffocated with smoke; consequently from Monday morning I anticipated with joy the approach of the next Sabbath, that I might again retire to the pleasant umbrage of the woods, whither I was used to dwell or spend the most of the day with ceaseless investigation over my book. A number strove to dissuade me from my plan, and had the presumption to tell me that I was a vain fool to attempt learning to read with as little chance as I had. Playboys importunately insisted on my abandoning my foolish theory, and go with them on streams, desport, and sacrifice the day in athletic folly, or alibatic levity. Nevertheless did I persevere with an indefatigable resolution, at the risk of success. But ah! the oppositions with which I contended are too tedious to relate, but not too formidable to surmount; and I verily believe that those obstacles had an auspicious tendency to waft me, as on pacific gales, above the storms of envy and the calumniating scourge of emulation, from which literary imagination often sinks beneath its dignity, and instruction languishes at the shrine of vanity. I reached the threatening heights of literature, and braved in a manner the clouds of disgust which reared in thunders under my feet. This brings to mind the verse of an author on the adventurous seaman.

"The wandering sailor ploughs the main,
A competence in life to gain;
The threatening waves around him foam,
'Till flattering fancy wafts him home."

For the overthrow and downfal of my scheme had been repeatedly threatened. But with defiance I accomplished the arduous task of spelling (for thus it was with me,) having no facilitating assistance. From this I entered into reading lessons with triumph. I became very fond of reading parts of the New Testament, such as I could pick up as they lay about at random; but I soon became more fond of reading verses, Wesley's old hymns, and other peices of poetry from various authors. I became found of it to that degree, that whenever I chanced to light on a piece of paper, so common to be lying about, I would pick it up in order to examine it whether it was written in that curious style or not. If it was not, unless some remarkable prose, I threw it aside; and if it was, I as carefully preserved it as I would a piece of money. At length I began to wonder whether it was possible that I ever could be so fortunate as to compose in that manner. I fell to work in my head, and composed several undigested pieces, which I retained in my mind, for I knew nothing about writing with a pen, also without the least grammatical knowledge, a few lines of which I yet retain. I will give you the following specimen. On one very calm Sabbath morning, a while before the time of preaching, I undertook to compose a divine hymn, being under some serious impression of mind:

Rise up, my soul and let us go
Up to the gospel feast;

Gird on the garment white as snow,
To join and be a guest.

Dost thou not hear the trumpet call
For thee, my soul, for thee?
Not only thee, my soul, but all,
May rise and enter free.

The other part I cannot now recollect. But in the course of some eight or ten months, under similar pensive impressions, I composed the following:

Excited from reading the obedience of Nature to her Lord in the vessel on the sea.

Master we perish if thou sleep,
We know not whence to fly;
The thunder seems to rock the deep,
Death frowns from all the sky.

He rose, he ran, and looking out,
He said, ye seas, be still;
What art thou, cruel storm about?
All silenced at his will.

Dost thou not know that thou art mine,

And all thy liquid stores;
Who ordered first the sun to shine
And gild thy swelling shores.

My smile is but the death of harm,
Whilst riding on the wind,
My power restrains the thunder's arm,
Which dies in chains confined.

After having read the travel of Israel from Egypt to the Red Red Sea, where they triumphantly arrive on the opposite bank, I was excited to compose the following few lines:

Sing, O ye ransom'd, shout and tell
What God has done for ye;
The horses and their riders fell
And perish'd in the sea.

Look back, the vain Egyptian dies
Whilst plunging from the shore;
He groans, he sinks, but not to rise,
King Pharaoh is no more.

Many other pieces did I compose, which have long since slipped my recollection, and some perhaps better than those before you. During this mental conflict no person was apprised of my views except my brother, who rather surmised it, being often in converse with me, and who was equally emulous for literatures and strove to rival me. Though he learnt to read very well for one of color, it seems that his genius did not direct him towards Parnassus, for he was rather a Josephus than a Homer; though he could write very well before I could form the first letter as above stated, for I devoted most of my opportunities to the study of composing or trying to compose. At any critical juncture, when any thing momentous transpired, such as death, misfortune, disappointment, and the like, it generally passed off from my mind like the chanting of birds after a storm, for my mind was then more deeply inspired than at other periods.

One thing is to be lamented much; that is, that ever I was raised in a family or neighborhood inclined to dissipation, or that the foul seed should have been sown in the bosom of youth, to stifle the growth of uncultivated genius, which like a torch lifted from a cell in the midst of rude inclement winds, which, instead of kindling its blaze, blows it out. My old master, being an eminent farmer, who had acquired a competent stock of living through his own prudence and industry, did not descend to the particularity of schooling his children at any high rate; hence it is clear that he cared less for the improvement of the mind of his servants. In fact, he was a man who aspired to a great deal of elaborate business, and carried me into measures almost beyond my physical ability. Often has he called me with my fellow laborers to his door to get the ordinary dram, of which he was much too fond himself; and we, willing to copy the example, partook freely in order to brave the storms of hardship, and thought it an honor to be intoxicated. And it was then the case with the most of people; for they were like savages, who think little or nothing of the result of lewd conduct. Nay, in those days, when the stream of intemperance was little regarded, the living had rather pour a libation on the bier of the plead than to hear a solemn funeral preached from the hallowed lips of a divine; for Bacchus was honored far more than Ceres, and they would rather impair the fences of fertile lands in their inebriating course than to assist a prudent farmer in cultivating a field for the space of an hour.

Those days resembled the days of martyrdom, and all christendom seemed to be relapsing into dissipation; and libertinism, obscenity and profanation were in their full career; and the common conversation was impregnated with droll blasphemy. In those days sensual gratification was prohibited by few; for drinking, I had almost said, was a catholic toleration, and from 1800 to 1810 there was scarcely a page of exemplary conduct laid before my eyes. Hence it was inevitably my misfortune to become a votary to that growing evil; and like a Saul, I was almost ready to hold the garments of an abominable rabble in their public sacrilege, to whom the tender of a book was offensive, especially to those who followed distilling on the Sabbath in the midst of a crowd of profligate sots, gambling around, regardless of demon, or Deity! Such scenes I have witnessed with any own eyes, when not a sunday school was planted in all the surrounding vicinities.

My old master having come to the conclusion to confer part of his servants on his children, lots were cast, and his son James fell heir to me. He was then living on Northampton, in the winter of 1814. In 1815 he moved into Chatham, when my opportunities became a little expanded. Having got in the way of carrying fruit to the college at Chapel Hill on the Sabbath, the collegians who, for their diversion, were fond of pranking with the country servants who resorted there for the same purpose that I did, began also to prank with me. But somehow or other they discovered a spark of genius in me, either by discourse or other means, which excited their curiosity, and they often eagerly insisted on me to spout, as they called it. This inspired in me a kind of enthusiastic pride I was indeed too full of vain egotism, which always discovers the gloom of ignorance, or dims the lustre of popular distinction. I would stand forth and address myself extempore before them, as an orator of inspired promptitude. But I soon found it an object of aversion, and considered myself nothing but a public ignoramus. Hence I abandoned my foolish harangues, and began to speak of poetry, which lifted these still higher on the wing of astonishment; all eyes were on me, and all ears were open. Many were at first incredulous; but the experiment of acrostics established it as an incontestable fact. Hence my fame soon circulated like a stream throughout the college. Many of these acrostics I composed at the handle of the plough, and retained them in my head, (being unable to write,) until an opportunity offered, when I dictated, whilst one of the gentlemen would serve as my emanuensis. I have composed love pieces in verse for courtiers from all parts of the state, and acrostics on the names of many of the tip top belles of Virginia, South Carolina and Georgia. But those criticising gentlemen saw plainly what I lacked, and many of them very generously gave me such books as they considered useful in my case, which I received with much gratitude, and improved according to my limited opportunities. Among, these gentlemen the following names occur to me: Mr. Robert Gilliam, Mr. Augustus Washington, Mr. Cornelius Roberson, Mr. Augustus Alston, Mr. Benjamin Long, Mr. William Harden, Mr. Merryfort, Mr. Augustus Moore, Mr. Thomas Pipkin, Mr. A. Rencher, Mr. Ellerbee, Mr. Gilmer, Mr. William Pickett, Mr. Leonidas Polk, Mr. Samuel Hinton, Mr. Pain, Mr. Steward, Mr. Gatlin, Mr. J. Hogan, Mr. John Pew, Messrs W. and J. Haywood, and several more whose names have slipped my memory; all of whom were equally liberal to me, and to them I ascribe my lean grammatical studies. Among the books given me were Murray's English Grammar and its accordant branches; Johnson's Dictionary in miniature, and also Walker's and Sheridan's, and parts of others. And other books of use they gave me, which I had no chance to peruse minutely. Milton's Paradise Lost, Thompson's Seasons, parts of Homer's Illiad and Virgil's Aenead, Beauties of Shakespear, Beauties of Byron, part of Plutarch, Morse's Geography, the Columbian Orator, Snowden's History of the Revolution, Young's Night Thoughts, and some others, which my concentration of business did not suffer me to pursue with any scientific regularity.

Mr. Augustus Alston first laid (as he said) the low price of twenty–five cents on my compositions each, which was unanimously established, and has been kept up ever since; but some gentlemen extremely generous, have given me from fifty to seventy–five cents, besides many decent and respectable suits of clothes, professing that they would not suffer me to pass otherwise and write for them.

But there is one thing with which I am sorry to charge many of these gentlemen. Before the moral evil of excessive drinking had been impressed upon my mind, they flattered me into the belief that it would hang me on the wings of new inspiration, which would waft me into regions of poetical perfection. And I am not a little astonished that nature and reason had not taught me better before, after having walked so long on a line which plainly dictated and read to me, though young, the lesson of human destruction. This realizes the truth of the sentiment in the address of the Earl of Chatham, in which he spoke of "the wretch who, after having seen the difficulties of a thousand errors, continues still to blunder;" and I have now experienced the destructive consequences of walking in such a devious line from the true centre to which I was so early attracted by–the magnet of genius. But I have discovered the beneficial effects of temperance and regularity, and fly as a penitent suppliant to the cell of private reflection, sorrowing that I ever had driven my boat of life so near the wrecking shoals of death, or that I was allured by the music of sirens that sing to ensnare the lovers of vanity.

To the much distinguished Mrs. Hentz of Boston, I owe much for the correction of many poetical errors. Being a professional poetess herself, and a lover of genius, she discovered my little uncultivated talent, and was moved by pity to uncover to me the beauties of correctness, together with the true importance of the object to which I aspired. She was extremely pleased with the dirge which I wrote on the death of her much lamented primogenial infant, and for which she gave me much credit and a handsome reward. Not being able to write myself, I dictated while she wrote; and while thus engaged she strove in vain to avert the inevitable tear slow trickling down her ringlet–shaded cheek. She was indeed unequivocally anxious to announce the birth of my recent and astonishing fame, and sent its blast on the gale of passage back to The frozen plains of Massachusetts.

This celebrated lady, however, did not continue long at Chapel Hill, and I had to regret the loss of her aid, which I shall never forget in life. As her departure from Chapel Hill, she left behind her the laurel of Thalia blooming on my mind, and went with all the spotless gaiety of Euphrosyne with regard to the signal services she had done me. In gratitude for all these favors, by which she attempted to supply and augment the stock of servile genius, I inscribe to her the following

EULOGY.
Deep on thy pillar, thou immortal dame,
Trace the inscription of eternal fame;
For bards unborn must yet thy works adore,
And bid thee live when others are no more.
When other names are lost among the dead,
Some genius yet may live thy fame to spread;
Memory's fair bush shall not decline to bloom,
But flourish fresh upon thy sacred tomb.
When nature's crown refuses to be gay,
And ceaseless streams have worn their rocks away;
When age's vail shall beauty's visage mask
And bid oblivion blot the poet's task,
Time's final shock shall elevate thy name,
And lift thee smiling to eternal fame.

I now commit my brief and blundering task to the inspection of the public, not pretending to warrant its philology nor its orthography, since grammarians, through criterions themselves, from precipitation do not always escape improprieties; and which little task, as before observed, I should not have assumed had it not been insisted on by some particular gentlemen, for I did not consider myself capable of such an undertaking. I trust, therefore, that my readers will rather pity than abuse the essay of their unqualified writer.

I will conclude with the following lines from the memorable pen of Mr. Linn, in which he has done honor to the cause of illiterate genius:

"Though in the dreary depth of gothic gloom,
Genius will burst the fetters of her tomb;
Yet education should direct her way,
And nerve with firmer grasp her powerful
sway."

INTRODUCTION.

The author of the following miscellaneous effusions, asserts that they are original, and recently written; and they are now presented to the test of criticism, whatever may be the result. It is entirely different from his other work entitled the Museum, and has been written some time since that, and is not so large. The author is far from flattering himself with an idea of superiority, or even equality with ancient or other modern poets. He is deeply conscious of his own inferiority from the narrowness of the scope in which he has lived during the course of his past life. Few men of either a white or colored population, have been less prompted by a desire for public fame than he whose productions are now before you. He was actuated merely by pleasure and curiosity, as a call to some literary task, or as an example to remove the doubts of cavilists with regard to African genius. His birth was low, and in a neighborhood by no means populous; his raising was rude and laborious; his exertions were cramped, and his progress obstructed from start to goal; having been ever deprived of the free use of books and other advantages to which he aspired. Hence his genius is but an unpolished diamond, and can never shine forth to the world.

Forbid to make the least attempt to soar, The stifled blaze of genius burns the more; He still prevails his drooping head to raise, Plods through the bogs, and on the mountains gaze.

THE MUSICAL CHAMBER.

I TRUST that my friends will remember,
Whilst I these my pleasures display,
Resort to my musical chamber,
The laurel crown'd desert in May.

Resort to this chamber at leisure,
Attend it by night and by day;
To feast on the dainties of pleasure,
Which cannot be stinted in May.

This place is both pleasing and moral,
A chamber both lovely and gay,
In the shade of a ne'er fading laurel,
Whose grace in December is May.

Abounding with every fine story,
While time passes hurrying away,
This place is a banquet of glory,
Which rings with the ditties of May.

The chamber of Chatham and Dolly,
A place of a comical play,
Gave place unto Lovel's fine folly,
The birds and sweet flowers of May.

Here Venus attends with her lover,

Here Floras their suitors betray,
And uncommon secrets discover,
Which break from the bosom of May.

Here ever young Hebe sits smiling,
The wonders of youth to portray,
Excluding old age from defiling
The lads and the lassies of May.

Call by, little stranger, one minute,
 Your joy will reward your delay;
Come, feast with the lark and the linnet,
And drink of the waters of May.

Walk in, little mistress, be steady,
You 'r welcome a visit to pay;
All things in the chamber are ready,
Resolve to be married in May.

A DIRGE.

Deserted of her Spouse, she sat lamenting in the chamber.

Hast thou gone and left me,
 Void of faults but strictly true?
Fly far away
Without delay,
Adieu, my love, adieu.

Hast thou gone and left me,
Hence to seek another bride?
I must be still,
Thou hast thy will,
The world is free and wide.

Only hadst thou told me
Ere I drunk the bitter cup,
I could with shame,

Now bear the blame,
And freely give thee up.

But I'm left to ponder,
Now in the depth of sorrow's gloom;
Like some dull sprite,
In dead of night,
Bewailing o'er her tomb.

Swiftly fly and welcome;
 It is the fate of fools to rove;
With whom I know
Wedlock is wo
Without the stream of love.

Where constant love is wanting,
Pleasure has not long to dwell;
I view my fate,
Alas, too late!
So partner, fare thee well.

But, my love, remember,
Hence we meet and face to face,
Thy heart shall ache,
Thy soul shall quake,
The wretch of all disgrace.

_____

DEATH OF A FAVORITE CHAMBER MAID.

O death, thy power I own,
Whose mission was to rush,
And snatch the rose, so quickly blown,
Down from its native bush;
The flower of beauty doom'd to pine,
Ascends from this to worlds divine.

Death is a joyful doom,
Let tears of sorrow dry,
The rose on earth but fades to bloom
And blossom in the sky.
Why should the soul resist the hand
That bears her to celestial land.

Then, bonny bird, farewell,
Till hence we meet again;
Perhaps I have not long to dwell
Within this cumb'rous chain,
Till on elysian shores eve meet,
Till grief is lost and joy complete.

THE FEARFUL TRAVELLER IN THE HAUNTED CASTLE.

Oft do I hear those windows ope
 And shut with dread surprise,
And spirits murmur as they grope,
But break not on the eyes.

Still fancy spies the winding sheet,
The phantom and the shroud,
And bids the pulse of horror beat
Throughout my ears aloud.

Some unknown finger thumps the door,
From one of faltering voice,
Till some one seems to walk the floor
With an alarming noise.

The drum of horror holds her sound,
Which will not let me sleep,
When ghastly breezes float around,
And hidden goblins creep.

Methinks I hear some constant groan,
The din of all the dead,
While trembling thus I lie alone,
Upon this restless bed.

At length the blaze of morning broke
On my impatient view,
And truth or fancy told the joke,
And bade the night adieu.

'Twas but the noise of prowling rats,
Which ran with all their speed,
Pursued in haste by hungry cats,
Which on the vermin feed.

The cat growl'd as she held her prey,
Which shriek'd with all its might,
And drove she balm of sleep away
Throughout the live–long night.

Those creatures crumbling off the cheese
Which on the table lay;
Some cats, too quick the rogues to seize,
With rumbling lost their prey.

Thus man is often his own elf,
Who makes the night his ghost,
And shrinks with horror from himself,
Which is to fear the most.

———————————

TO CATHARINE.

I'll love thee as along as I live,
Whate'er thy condition may be;
All else but my life would I give,

That thou wast as partial to me.

I love thee because thou art fair,
  And fancy no other beside;
I languish thy pleasures to share,
Whatever my life may betide.

I'll love thee when youth's vital beam
Grows dim on the visage of cares;
And trace back on time's rapid stream,
Thy beauty when sinking in years.

Though nature no longer is gay,
  With blooms which the simple adore,
Let virtue forbid me to say,
That Cath'rine is lovely no more.

THE SWAN —VAIN PLEASURES.

The Swan which boasted mid the tide,
Whose nest was guarded by the wave,
Floated for pleasure till she died,
And sunk beneath the flood to lave.

The bird of fashion drops her wing,
The rose—bush now declines to bloom;
The gentle breezes of the spring
No longer waft a sweet perfume.

Fair beauty with those lovely eyes,
Withers along her vital stream;
Proud fortune leaves her throne, and flies
From pleasure, as a flattering dream.

The eagle of exalted fame,

Which spreads his pinions far to sail,
Struggled to fan his dying flame,
Till pleasure pall'd in every gale.

And gaudy mammon, sordid gain,
Whose plume has faded, once so gay,
Languishes mid her flowery train,
Whilst pleasure flies like fumes away.

Vain pleasures, O how short to last!
Like leaves which quick to ashes burn;
Which kindle from the slightest blast,
And slight to nothing hence return.

THE POWERS OF LOVE.

It lifts the poor man from his cell
To fortune's bright alcove;
Its mighty sway few, few can tell,
Mid envious foes it conquers ill;
There's nothing half like love.

Ye weary strangers, void of rest,
Who late through life have strove,
Like the late bird which seeks its nest,
If you would hence in truth be blest,
Light on the bough of love.

The vagrant plebeian, void of friends,
Constrain'd through wilds to rove,
On this his safety whole depends,
One faithful smile his trouble ends,
A smile of constant love.

Thus did a captured wretch complain,
  Imploring heaven above,

Till one with sympathetic pain,
Flew to his arms and broke the chain,
 And grief took flight from love.

Let clouds of danger rise and roar,
And hope's firm pillars move;
With storms behind and death before,
 O grant me this, I crave no more,
There's nothing half like love.

When nature wakes soft pity's coo
The hawk deserts the dove,
Compassion melts the creature through,
With palpitations felt by few,
The wrecking throbs of love.

Let surly discord take its flight
From wedlock's peaceful grove,
While union breaks the arm of fight,
With darkness swallow'd up in light,
O what is there like love.

TO A DEPARTING FAVORITE.

Thou mayst retire, but think of me
When thou art gone afar,
Where'er in life thy travels be,
If tost along the brackish sea,
Or borne upon the car.

Thou mayst retire, I care not where,
Thy name my theme shall be;
With thee in heart I shall be there,
Content thy good or ill to share,
If dead to lodge with thee.

Thou mayst retire beyond the deep,
 And leave thy sister train,
To roam the wilds where dangers sleep,
And leave affection sad to weep
In bitterness and pain.

Thou mayst retire, and yet be glad
To leave me thus alone,
Lamenting and bewailing sad;
Farewell, thy sunk deluded lad
May rise when thou art gone.

THE TRAVELLER.

'Tis sweet to think of home.

When from my native clime,
Mid lonely vallies pensive far I roam,
Mid rocks and hills where waters roll sublime,
'Tis sweet to think of home.

My retrospective gaze
Bounds on a dark horizon far behind,
But yet the stars of homely pleasures blaze
And glimmer on my mind.

When pealing thunders roll,
And ruffian winds howl, threat'ning life with gloom,
To Heaven's kind hand I then commit the whole,
And smile to think of home.

But cease, my pensive soul,
To languish at departure's gloomy shrine;
Still look in front and hail the joyful goal,
The pleasure teeming line.

When on the deep wide sea
I wander, sailing mid the swelling foam,
Tost from the land by many a long degree,
O, then I think of thee.

I never shall forget
The by-gone pleasures of my native shore,
Until the sun of life forbears to set,
And pain is known no more.

When nature seems to weep,
And life hangs trembling o'er the watery tomb,
Hope lifts her peaceful sail to brave the deep,
And bids me think of home.

My favorite pigeon rest,
Nor on the plane of sorrow drop thy train,
But on the bough of hope erect thy nest,
Till friends shall meet again.

Though in the hermit's cell,
Where eager friends to cheer me fail to come,
Where Zeph'rus seems a joyless tale to tell,
No thought is sweet but home.

RECENT APPEARANCE OF A LADY.

The joy of meeting one so fair,
Inspires the present stream of song;
A bonny belle,
That few excell,
And one with whom I few compare,
Though out of sight so long.

It is a cause of much delight,

When lads and lasses meet again;
But, bonny belle,
No long to dwell,
For soon, upon the wing of flight,
We haste away in pain.

That long hid form I smile to trace,
A star emerging out of gloom,
Exalted belle,
Whose powers impell,
And draw the heart by every grace,
The queen of every bloom.

Long out of sight, but still in mind,
Eternal me'mry holds its grasp,
Still, bonny belle,
'Tis sweet to tell
Of thee, when I am left behind
In sorrow's lonely clasp.

MEDITATION ON A COLD, DARK, AND RAINY NIGHT.

Sweet on the house top falls the gentle shower,
When jet black darkness crowns the silent hour,
 When shrill the owlet pours her hollow tone,
Like some lost child sequester'd and alone,
When Will's bewildering wisp begins to flare,
And Philomela breathes her dulcet air,
'Tis sweet to listen to her nightly tune,
Deprived of star—light or the smiling moon.
When deadly winds sweep round the rural shed,
And tell of strangers lost, without a bed,
Fond sympathy invokes her dol'rous lay,
 And pleasure steals in sorrow's gloom away,
Till fost'ring Somnus bids my eyes to close,
And smiling visions open to repose;
Still on my soothing couch I lie at ease,
Still round my chamber flows the whistling breeze,
Still in the chain of sleep I lie confined,

To all the threat'ning ills of life resign'd,
Regardless of the wand'ring elfe of night,
While phantoms break on my immortal sight.
The trump of morning bids my slumbers end,
While from a flood of rest I straight ascend,
When on a busy world I cast my eyes,
And think of nightly slumbers with surprise.

ON AN OLD DELUDED SUITOR.

See sad deluded love, in years too late,
With tears desponding o'er the tomb of fate,
While dusky evening's veil excludes the light
Which in the morning broke upon his sight.
He now regrets his vain, his fruitless plan,
And sadly wonders at the faults of man.
'Tis now from beauty's torch he wheels aside,
And strives to soar above affection's tide;
'Tis now that sorrow feeds the worm of pain
With tears which never can the loss regain;
'Tis now he drinks the wormwood and the gall,
And all the sweets of early pleasures pall,
When from his breast the hope of fortune flies,
The songs of transport languish into sighs;
Fond, lovely rose, that beamed as she blew,
Of all the charms of youth the most untrue,
She, with delusive smiles, prevail'd to move
This silly heart into the snare of love;
Then like a flower closed against the bee,
Folds her arms and turns her back on me.
When on my fancy's eye her smiles she shed,
The torch by which deluded love was led,
Then, like a lark, from boyhood's maze I soar'd,
And thus in song her flattering smiles adored.
My heart was then by fondling love betray'd,
A thousand pleasures bloom'd but soon to fade,
From joy to joy my heart exulting flew,
In quest of one, though fair, yet far from true.

THE WOODMAN AND MONEY HUNTER.

Throughout our rambles much we find;
The bee trees burst with honey;
Wild birds we tame of every kind,
At once they seem to be resign'd;
I know but one that lags behind,
There's nothing lags but money.

The woods afford us much supply,
The opossum, coon, and coney;
They all are tame and venture nigh,
Regardless of the public eye,
I know but one among them shy,
There's nothing shy but money.

And she lies in the bankrupt shade;
The cunning fox is funny;
When thus the public debts are paid,
Deceitful cash is not afraid,
Where funds are hid for private trade,
There's nothing paid but money.

Then let us roam the woods along,
And drive the coon and coney;
Our lead is good, our powder strong,
To shoot the pigeons as they throng,
But sing no more the idle song,
Nor prowl the chase for money.

THE EYE OF LOVE.

I know her story—telling eye
Has more expression than her tongue;
And from that heart—extorted sigh,
At once the peal of love is rung.

When that soft eye lets fall a tear

Of doating fondness as we part,
The stream is from a cause sincere,
And issues from a melting heart.

What shall her fluttering pulse restrain,
The life—watch beating from her soul,
When all the power of hate is slain,
And love permits it no control.

When said her tongue, I wish thee well,
Her eye declared it must be true;
And every sentence seem'd to tell
The tale of sorrow told by few.

When low she bow'd and wheel'd aside,
I saw her blushing temples fade;
Her smiles were sunk in sorrow's tide,
But love was in her eye betray'd.

THE SETTING SUN.

'Tis sweet to trace the setting sun
Wheel blushing down the west;
When his diurnal race is run,
The traveller stops the gloom to shun,
And lodge his bones to rest.

Far from the eye he sinks apace,
But still throws back his light
From oceans of resplendent grace,
Whence sleeping vesper paints her face,
And bids the sun good night.

To those hesperian fields by night
My thoughts in vision stray,
Like spirits stealing into light,
From gloom upon the wing of flight,
Soaring from time away.

Our eagle, with his pinions furl'd,
Takes his departing peep,
And hails the occidental world,
Swift round whose base the globes are whirl'd,
Whilst weary creatures sleep.

THE RISING SUN.

The king of day rides on,
To give the placid morning birth;
On wheels of glory moves his throne,
Whose light adorns the earth.

When once his limpid maid
Has the imperial course begun,
The lark deserts the dusky glade,
And soars to meet the sun.

Up from the orient deep,
Aurora mounts without delay,
With brooms of light the plains to sweep,
And purge the gloom away.

Ye ghostly scenes give way,
 Our king is coming now in sight,
Bearing the diadem of day,
Whose crest expels the night.

Thus we, like birds, retreat
To groves, and hide from ev'ry eye;
Our slumb'ring dust will rise and meet
Its morning in the sky.

The immaterial sun,
Now hid within empyreal gloom,
Will break forth on a brighter throne,
And call us from the tomb.

23

MEMORY.

Sweet memory, like a pleasing dream,
 Still lends a dull and feeble ray;
For ages with her vestige teems,
When beauty's trace is worn away.

When pleasure, with her harps unstrung,
Sits silent to be heard no more,
Or leaves them on the willows hung,
And pass—time glee forever o'er;

Still back in smiles thy glory steals
With ev'ning dew drops from thine eye;
The twilight bursting from thy wheels,
Ascends and bids oblivion fly.

Memory, thy bush prevails to bloom,
Design'd to fade, no, never, never,
Will stamp thy vestige on the tomb,
And bid th' immortal live forever.

When youth's bright sun has once declined
And bid his smiling day expire,
Mem'ry, thy torch steals up behind,
And sets thy hidden stars on fire.

PROSPERITY.

Come, thou queen of every creature,
Nature calls thee to her arms ;

Love sits gay on every feature,
Teeming with a thousand charms.

Meet me mid the wreathing bowers,
Greet me in the citron grove,
Where I saw the belle of flowers
Dealing with the blooms of love.

Hark! the lowly dove of Sharon,
Bids thee rise and come away,
From a vale both dry and barren,
Come to one where life is gay.

Come, thou queen of all the forest,
Fair Feronia, mountain glee,
Lovelier than the garden florist,
Or the goddess of the bee.

Come, Sterculus, and with pleasure,
Fertilize the teeming field;
From thy straw, dissolved at leisure,
Bid the lea her bounty yield.

Come, thou queen of every creature,
Nature calls thee to her arms;
Love sits gay on every feature,
Teeming with a thousand charms.

———————

DEATH OF GEN. JACKSON —AN EULOGY.

Hark! from the mighty Hero's tomb,
I hear a voice proclaim!
A sound which fills the world with gloom,
But magnifies his name.

His flight from time let braves deplore,
And wail from state to state,
And sound abroad from shore to shore,
The death of one so great!

He scorn'd to live a captured slave,
And fought his passage through;
He dies, the prince of all the brave,
And bids the world adieu!

Sing to the mem'ry of his power,
Ye vagrant mountaineers,
Ye rustic peasants drop a shower
Of love for him in tears.

He wields the glittering sword no more,
With that transpiercing eye;
Ceases to roam the mountain o'er,
And gets him down to die!

Still let the nation spread his fame,
While marching from his tomb;
Aloud let all the world proclaim,
Jackson, forever bloom.

No longer to the world confin'd,
He goes down like a star;
He sets, and leaves his friends behind
To rein the steed of war.

Hark! from the mighty Hero's tomb,
I hear a voice proclaim!
A sound which fills the world with gloom,
But magnifies his name!

MR. CLAY'S RECEPTION AT RALEIGH,

April, 1844.

Salute the august train! a scene so grand,
With every tuneful band;
The mighty brave,
His country bound to save,
Extends his aiding hand;
For joy his vot'ries hoop and stamp,
Excited by the blaze of pomp!
Let ev'ry eye
The scene descry,
The sons of freedom's land.

They look ten thousand stars! lamp tumbler blaze,
To give the Hero praise!
Immortal Clay,
The cause is to pourtray!
Your tuneful voices raise;
The lights of our Columbian sun,
Break from his patriotic throne;
Let all admire
The faithful sire,
The chief musician plays.

Ye bustling crowds give way, proclaims the drum,
And give the Patriot room;
The cannon's sound,
The blast of trumpets bound,
Be this our father's home;
Now let the best musician play,
A skillful tune for Henry Clay!
Let every ear
With transport hear!
The President is come.

Let sister states greet the Columbian feast,
With each admiring guest;
Thou art our choice!
Let ev'ry joyful voice,

Sound from the east to west;
Let haughty Albion's lion roar,
The eagle must prevail to soar;
And in lovely form,
Above the storm,
Erect her peaceful nest.

Beyond each proud empire she throws her eye!
Which lifted to the sky,
No thunders roll,
To agitate her soul,
Beneath her feet they fly!
Let skillful fingers sweep the lyre,
Strike ev'ry ear! set hearts on fire!
Let monarchs sleep
Beyond the deep,
And howling faction die.

Nor hence forget the scene applauding day,
When every heart was gay;
The universal swell
Rush'd from the loud town bell;
In awful, grand array,
We see them form the bright parade;
And hark, a gladdening march is play'd!
Along the street,
The theme is sweet,
For every voice is Clay.

To the Capitol the low and upland peers
Resort with princely fears,
And homage pay;
A loud huzza for Clay!
Falls on our ears;
Loud from his lips the thunders roll,
And fill with wonder every soul;
Round the sire of state
All concentrate,
And every mortal hears.

———————

CLAY'S DEFEAT.

'Tis the hope of the noble defeated;
The aim of the marksman is vain;
The wish of destruction completed,
The soldier eternally slain.

When winter succeeds to the summer,
The bird is too chilly to sing;
No music is play'd for the drummer,
No carol is heard on the wing.

The court of a nation forsaken,
An edifice stripp'd of its dome,
Its fame from her pinnacle shaken,
Like the sigh heaving downfall of Rome.

Fall'n, fall'n is the chief of the witty,
The prince of republican power;
The star–crown of Washington City
Descends his political tower.

The gold–plated seat is bespoken,
The brave of the west is before;
The bowl at the fountain is broken,
The music of fame is no more.

No longer a wonderful story
Is told for the brave whig to hear,
Whose sun leaves his circuit of glory,
Or sinks from the light of his sphere.

THE HAPPY BIRD'S NEST.

When on my cottage falls the placid shower,
When ev'ning calls the labourer home to rest,
When glad the bee deserts the humid flower,

O then the bird assumes her peaceful nest.

When sable shadows grow unshapely tall,
And Sol's resplendent wheel descends the west,
The knell of respiration tolls for all,
And Hesper smiles upon the linnet's nest.

When o'er the mountain bounds the fair gazell,
The night bird tells her day–departing jest,
She gladly leaves her melancholy dell,
 And spreads her pinions o'er the linnet's nest.

Then harmless Dian spreads her lucid sail,
 And glides through ether with her silver crest,
Bidding the watchful bird still pour her tale,
And cheer the happy linnet on her nest.

Thus may some guardian angel bear her light,
And o'er thy tomb, departed genius, rest,
Whilst thou shalt take thy long eternal flight,
And leave some faithful bird to guard thy nest.

THE FATE OF AN INNOCENT DOG.

When Tiger left his native yard,
He did not many ills regard,
A fleet and harmless cur;
Indeed, he was a trusty dog,
And did not through the pastures prog;
The grazing flocks to stir, poor dog,
The grazing flocks to stir.

He through a field by chance was led,
In quest of game not far ahead,
And made one active leap;
When all at once, alarm'd, he spied,

A creature welt'ring on its side,
A deadly wounded sheep, alas!
A deadly wounded sheep.

He there was fill'd with sudden fear,
Apprized of lurking danger near,
And there he left his trail;
Indeed, he was afraid to yelp,
Nor could he grant the creature help,
But wheel'd and drop'd his tail, poor dog,
But wheel'd and drop'd his tail.

It was his pass—time, pride and fun,
At morn the nimble hare to run,
When frost was on the grass;
Returning home who should he meet?
The weather's owner, coming fleet,
Who scorn'd to let him pass, alas!
Who scorn'd to let him pass.

Tiger could but his bristles raise,
A surly compliment he pays,
Insulted shows his wrath;
Returns a just defensive growl,
And does not turn aside to prowl,
But onward keeps the path, poor dog,
But onward keeps the path.

The raging owner found the brute,
But could afford it no recruit,
Nor raise it up to stand;
'Twas mangled by some other dogs,
A set of detrimental rogues,
Raised up at no command, alas!
Raised up at no command.

Sagacious Tiger left his bogs,
But bore the blame of other dogs,
With powder, fire and ball;
They kill'd the poor, unlawful game,

And then came back and eat the same ;
But Tiger paid for all, poor dog,
But Tiger paid for all.

Let ev'ry harmless dog beware
Lest he be taken in the snare,
And scorn such fields to roam;
A creature may be fraught with grace,
And suffer for the vile and base,
By straggling off from home, alas!
By straggling off from home.

The blood of creatures oft is spilt,
Who die without a shade of guilt;
Look out, or cease to roam;
Whilst up and down the world he plays
For pleasure, man in danger strays
Without a friend from home, alas!
Without a friend from home.

THE TIPLER TO HIS BOTTLE.

What hast thou ever done for me?
Defeated every good endeavor;
I never can through life agree
To place my confidence in thee,
Not ever, no, never!

Often have I thy steam admired,
Thou nothing hast avail'd me ever;
 Vain have I thought myself inspired,
Say, have I else but pain acquired?
Not ever, no, never!

No earthly good, no stream of health,
Flows from thy fount, thou cheerful giver;
From thee, affluence sinks to stealth,
From thee I pluck no bloom of health,
Whatever, no, never!

Thou canst impart a nobel mind,
Power from my tongue flows like a river;
The gas flows dead, I'm left behind,
To all that's evil down confined,
To flourish more never!

With thee I must through life complain,
Thy powers at large will union sever;
Disgorge no more thy killing bane,
The bird hope flies from thee in pain,
To return more never!

ROSABELLA—PURITY OF HEART.

Though with an angel's tongue
I set on fire the congregations all,
'Tis but a brazen bell that I have rung,
And I to nothing fall;
My theme is but an idle air
If Rosabella is not there,

Though I in thunders rave,
And hurl the blaze of oratoric flowers,
Others I move, but fail myself to save
With my declaiming powers;
I sink, alas! I know not where,
If Rosabella is not there.

Though I point out the way,
And closely circumscribe the path to heaven,
And pour my melting prayer without delay,
And vow my sins forgiven,
I sink into the gloom despair
If Rosabella is not there,

Though I may mountains move,

And make the vallies vocal with my song,
I'm vain without a stream of mystic love,
For all my heart is wrong;
I've laid myself a cruel snare,
If Rosabella is not there.

From bibliothic stores,
I fly, proclaiming heaven from land to land,
Or cross the seas and reach their distant shores,
Mid Gothic groups to stand;
O, let me of myself beware,
If Rosabella is not there.

Our classic books must fail,
And with their flowery tongues to ashes burn,
And not one groat a mortal wit avail
Upon his last return;
Be this the creature's faithful prayer,
That Rosabella may be there.

This spotless maid was born
The babe of heaven, and cannot be defiled;
The soul is dead and in a state forlorn
On which she has not smiled;
Vain are the virile and the fair,
If Rosabella be not there.

When other pleasures tire,
And mortal glories fade to glow no more,
She with the wings of truth augments her fire,
And still prevails to soar;
All else must die, the good and wise,
But Rosabella never dies.

FALSE WEIGHT.

The poor countryman to a fraudulent lady professing bright christianity.

If thou art fair, deal, lady, fair,
And let the scales be even;
Forbid the poising beam to rear,
And pull thee down from heaven.

Dost thou desire to die in peace,
For ev'ry sin forgiven,
Give back my right, thy weight decrease,
And mount like mine to heaven.

Rather give over to the poor,
Take ten and give eleven;
Or else be fair, I ask no more,
'Tis all required of heaven.

And when on thee for pay I call,
Which is but four for seven,
Keep nothing back, but pay it all,
It is not hid from heaven.

Remember hence the sentence past,
The truth in scripture given,
Last shall be first, and first be last,
In time, in earth, and heaven.

———————————

DEPARTING SUMMER.

When auburn Autumn mounts the stage,
And Summer fails her charms to yield,
Bleak nature turns another page,
To light the glories of the field.

At once the vale declines to bloom,
The forest smiles no longer gay;
Gardens are left without perfume,

The rose and lilly pine away.

The orchard bows her fruitless head,
As one divested of her store;
Or like a queen whose train has fled,
And left her sad to smile no more.

That bird which breath'd her vernal song,
And hopp'd along the flow'ry spray,
Now silent holds her warbling tongue,
Which dulcifies the feast of May.

But let each bitter have its sweet,
No change of nature is in vain;
'Tis just alternate cold and heat,
For time is pleasure mix'd with pain.

———————

REFLECTIONS FROM THE FLASH OF A METEOR.

Psalm xc. 12.

So teach me to regard my day,
How small a point my life appears;
One gleam to death the whole betrays,
A momentary flash of years.

One moment smiles, the scene is past,
Life's gaudy bloom at once we shed,
And thinly beneath affliction's blast,
Or drop as soon among the dead.

Short is the chain wound up at morn,
Which oft runs down and stops at noon;
Thus in a moment man is born,
And, lo! the creature dies as soon.

Life's little torch how soon forgot,
Dim burning on its dreary shore;
Just like that star which downwards shot,
It glimmers and is seen no more.

Teach me to draw this transient breath,
With conscious awe my end to prove,
Early to make my peace with death,
As thus in haste from time we move.

O heaven, through this murky vale,
Direct me with a burning pen;
Thus shall I on a tuneful gale
Fleet out my threescore years and ten.

TRUE FRIENDSHIP.

Friendship, thou balm for ev'ry ill,
I must aspire to thee;
Whose breezes bid the heart be still,
And render sweet the patient's pill,
And set the pris'ner free.

Friendship, it is the softest soul
Which feels another's pain;
And must with equal sighs condole,
While sympathetic streamlets roll,
Which nothing can restrain.

Not to be nominated smart,
Of mortals to be seen,
She does not thus her gifts impart,
Her aid is from a feeling heart,
A principle within.

When the lone stranger, forced to roam,
Comes shiv'ring to her door,
At once he finds a welcome home,
The torch of grace dispels his gloom,
And bids him grope no more.

Friendship was never known to fail
The voice of need to hear,
When ruthless ills our peace assail,
When from our hearts she draws the veil,
And drys the falling tear.

When dogs and devils snarl and fight,
She hides and dwells alone;
When friends and kindred disunite,
With pity she surveys the right,
And gives to each his own.

Friendship has not a sister grace
Her wonders to exceed;
She is the queen of all her race,
Whose charms the stoutest must embrace
When in the vale of need.

Friendship is but the feeling sigh,
The sympathizing tear,
Constrain'd to flow till others dry,
Nor lets the needy soul pass by,
Nor scorns to see or hear.

———————————

ON THE CONVERSION OF A SISTER.

'Tis the voice of my sister at home,
Resign'd to the treasures above,
Inviting the strangers to come,
And feast at the banquet of love.

'Tis a spirit cut loose from its chain,
'Tis the voice of a culprit forgiven,
Restored from a prison of pain,
With th' sound of a concert from heaven.

'Tis a beam from the regions of light,
A touch of beatific fire;
A spirit exulting for flight,
With a strong and impatient desire.

'Tis a drop from the ocean of love,
A foretaste of pleasures to come,
Distill'd from the fountain above,
The joy which awaits her at home.

A BILLET DOUX.

DEAR MISS: Notwithstanding the cloud of doubts which overshadows the mind of adoring fancy, when I trace that vermillion cheek, that sapphire eye of expressive softness, and that symmetrical form of grace, I am constrained to sink into a flood of admiration beneath those heavenly charms. Though, dear Miss, it may be useless to introduce a multiplicity of blandishments, which might either lead you into a field of confusion, or absorb the truth of affection in the gloom of doubts; but the bell of adulation may be told from the distance of its echo, and cannot be heard farther than seen. Dear Miss, whatever may be the final result of my adventurous progress, I now feel a propensity to embark on the ocean of chance, and expand the sail of resolution in quest of the distant shore of connubial happiness with one so truly lovely. Though, my dearest, the thunders of parental aversion may inflect the guardian index of affection from its favorite star, the deviated needle recovers its course, and still points onwards to its native poll. Though the waves of calumny may reverberate the persevering mind of the sailing lover, the morning star of hope directs him through the gloom of trial to the object of his choice.

My brightest hopes are mix'd with tears,
Like hues of light and gloom;
As when mid sun—shine rain appears,
Love rises with a thousand fears,

To pine and still to bloom.
When I have told my last fond tale
In lines of song to thee,

And for departure spread my sail,
Say, lovely princess, wilt thou fail
To drop a tear for me?

O, princess, should my votive strain
Salute thy ear no more,
Like one deserted on the main,
I still shall gaze, alas! but vain,
On wedlock's flow'ry shore.

TROUBLED WITH THE ITCH, AND RUBBING WITH SULPHUR.

'Tis bitter, yet 'tis sweet,
Scratching effects but transient ease;
Pleasure and pain together meet,
And vanish as they please.

My nails, the only balm,
To ev'ry bump are oft applied,
And thus the rage will sweetly calm
Which aggravates my hide.

It soon returns again;
A frown succeeds to ev'ry smile;
Grinning I scratch and curse the pain,
But grieve to be so vile.

In fine, I know not which
Can play the most deceitful game,
The devil, sulphur, or the itch;
The three are but the same.

The devil sows the itch,
And sulphur has a loathsome smell,
And with my clothes as black as pitch,

I stink where'er I dwell.

Excoriated deep,
By friction play'd on ev'ry part,
It oft deprives me of my sleep,
And plagues me to my heart.

EARLY AFFECTION.

I loved thee from the earliest dawn,
When first I saw thy beauty's ray;
And will until life's eve comes on,
And beauty's blossom fades away;
And when all things go well with thee,
With smiles or tears remember me.

I'll love thee when thy morn is past
And wheedling galantry is o'er,
When youth is lost in age's blast,
And beauty can ascend no more;
And when life's journey ends with thee,
O then look back and think of me.

I'll love thee with a smile or frown,
Mid sorrow's gloom or pleasure's light;
And when the chain of life runs down,
Pursue thy last eternal flight;
When thou hast spread thy wing to flee,
Still, still a moment wait for me.

I love thee for those sparkling eyes,
To which my fondness was betray'd,
Bearing the tincture of the skies,
To glow when other beauties fade;
And when they sink too low to see,
 Reflect an azure beam on me.

THE CREDITOR TO HIS PROUD DEBTOR.

Ha, tott'ring Johny, strut and boast,
But think of what your feathers cost;
Your crowing days are short at most,
You bloom but soon to fade;
Surely you could not stand so wide,
If strictly to the bottom tried,
The wind would blow your plume aside
If half your debts were paid.
Then boast and bear the crack,
With the sheriff at your back;
Huzza for dandy Jack,
My jolly fop, my Joe.

The blue smoke from your segar flies,
Offensive to my nose and eyes;
The most of people would be wise
Your presence to evade;
Your pocket jingles loud with cash,
And thus you cut a foppish dash,
But, alas! dear boy, you would be trash,
If your accounts were paid.
Then boast and bear the crack, &c.

My duck bill boots would look as bright,
Had you in justice served me right;
Like you I then could step as light,
Before a flaunting maid;
As nicely could I clear my throat,
And to my tights my eyes devote;
But I'd leave you bare without that coat,
 For which you have not paid.
Then boast and bear the crack, &c.

I'd toss myself with a scornful air,
And to a poor man pay no care;
I could rock cross–leg'd on my chair
Within the cloister shade;
I'd gird my neck with a light cravat,
And creaning wear my bell–crown hat;

But away my down would fly at that,
If once my debts were paid.
 Then boast and bear the crack,
With a sheriff at your back;
Huzza for dandy Jack,
My jolly fop, my Joe.

———————————

REGRET FOR THE DEPARTURE OF FRIENDS.

As smoke from a volcano soars in the air,
The soul of man discontent mounts from a sigh,
Exhaled as to heaven in mystical prayer,
Invoking that love which forbids him to die.

Sweet hope, lovely passion, my grief ever chase,
And scatter the gloom which veils pleasure's bright ray,
O lend me thy wings, and assist me to trace
The flight of my fair one when gone far away.

When the dim star of pleasure sets glimmering alone,
The planet of beauty on life's dreary shore,
And th' fair bird of fancy forever is flown,
On pinions of haste to be heard of no more.

Hope, tell me, dear passion, thou wilt not forget,
To flourish still sweetly and blossom as gay,
Expelling like morning the gloom of regret,
When the lark of affection is gone far away.

If hurried into some unchangeable clime,
Where oceans of pleasure continually roll,
Far, far from the limited borders of time,
With a total division of body and soul.

Hope, tell me, dear passion, which must earth survive,

43

That love will be sweeter when nature is o'er,
And still without pain though eternity live,
In the triumph of pleasure when time is no more.

O love, when the day—light of pleasure shall close,
Let the vesper of death break on life's dusky even;
Let the faint sun of time set in peace as it rose,
And eternity open thy morning in heaven.

Then hope, lovely passion, thy torch shall expire,
Effusing on nature life's last feeble ray;
While the night maid of love sets her taper on fire,
To guard smiling beauty from time far away.

FAREWELL TO FRANCES.

Farewell! if ne'er I see thee more,
Though distant calls my flight impel,
I shall not less thy grace adore,
So friend, forever fare thee well.

Farewell! forever, did I say?
What, never more thy face to see?
Then take the last fond look to—day,
And still to—morrow think of me.

Farewell! alas, the tragic sound
Has many a tender bosom torn;
While desolation spread around,
Deserted friendship left to mourn.

Farewell! awakes the sleeping tear,
The dormant rill from sorrow's eye,
Express'd from one by nature dear,
Whose bosom heaves the latent sigh.

Farewell! is but departure's tale,
When fond association ends,
And fate expands her lofty sail,
To show the distant flight of friends.

Alas! and if we sure must part,
Far separated long to dwell,
I leave thee with a broken heart,
So friend, forever, fare thee well.

I leave thee, but forget thee never,
Words cannot my feeling tell,
"Fare thee well, and if forever,
Still forever fare thee well."

THE RETREAT FROM MOSCOW.

Sad Moscow, thy fate do I see,
Fire! fire! in the city all cry;
Like quails from the eagle all flee,
Escape in a moment or die.

It looks like the battle of Troy,
The storm rises higher and higher;
The scene of destruction all hearts must annoy,
The whirlwinds, the smoke, and the fire.

The dread conflagration rolls forth,
Augmenting the rage of the wind,
Which blows it from south unto north,
And leaves but the embers behind.

It looks like Gomorrah; the flame
Is moving still nigher and nigher,
Aloud from all quarters the people proclaim,

The whirlwinds, the smoke, and the fire.

A dead fumigation now swells,
A blue circle darkens the air,
With tones as the pealing of bells,
Farewell to the brave and the fair.

O Moscow, thou city of grace,
Consign'd to a dread burning pyre,
From morning to ev'ning with sorrow I trace
The wild winds, the smoke, and the fire.

The dogs in the kennel all howl,
The wether takes flight with the ox,
Appal'd on the wing is the fowl,
The pigeon deserting her box.

With a heart full of pain, in the night
Mid hillocks and bogs I retire,
Through lone, deadly vallies I steer by its light,
The wild storm, the smoke, and the fire.

Though far the crash breaks on my ear,
The stars glimmer dull in the sky,
The shrieks of the women I hear,
The fall of the kingdom is nigh.

O heaven, when earth is no more,
And all things in nature expire,
May I thus, with safety, keep distant before
The whirlwinds, the smoke, and the fire.

IMPLORING TO BE RESIGNED AT DEATH.

Let me die and not tremble at death,
But smile at the close of my day,
And then, at the flight of my breath,

Like a bird of the morning in May,
Go chanting away.

Let me die without fear of the dead,
No horrors my soul shall dismay,
And with faith's pillow under my head,
With defiance to mortal decay,
Go chanting away.

Let me die like a son of the brave,
And martial distinction display,
Nor shrink from a thought of the grave,
No, but with a smile from the clay,
Go chanting away.

Let me die glad, regardless of pain,
No pang to this world to betray;
And the spirit cut loose from its chain,
So loath in the flesh to delay,
Go chanting away.

Let me die, and my worst foe forgive,
When death veils the last vital ray;
Since I have but a moment to live,
Let me, when the last debt I pay,
Go chanting away.

ON THE PLEASURES OF COLLEGE LIFE.

With tears I leave these academic bowers,
And cease to cull the scientific flowers;
With tears I hail the fair succeeding train,
And take my exit with a breast of pain.
The Fresh may trace these wonders as they smile;
The stream of science like the river Nile,
Reflecting mental beauties as it flows,
Which all the charms of College life disclose;

This sacred current as it runs refines,
Whilst Byron sings and Shakspeare's mirror shines.
 First like a garden flower did I rise,
When on the college bloom I cast my eyes;
I strove to emulate each smiling gem,
Resolved to wear the classic diadem;
But when the Freshman's garden breeze was gone;
Around me spread a vast extensive lawn;
'Twas there the muse of college life begun,
Beneath the rays of erudition's sun,
Where study drew the mystic focus down,
And lit the lamp of nature with renown;
There first I heard the epic thunders roll,
And Homer's light'ning darted through my soul.
Hard was the task to trace each devious line,
Though Locke and Newton bade me soar and shine;
I sunk beneath the heat of Franklin's blaze,
And struck the notes of philosophic praise;
With timid thought I strove the test to stand,
Reclining on a cultivated land,
Which often spread beneath a college bower,
And thus invoked the intellectual shower;
E'en that fond sire on whose depilous crown,
The smile of courts and states shall shed renown;
Now far above the noise of country strife,
I frown upon the gloom of rustic life,
Where no pure stream of bright distinction flows,
No mark between the thistle and the rose;
One's like a bird encaged and bare of food,
Borne by the fowler from his native wood,
Where sprightly oft he sprung from spray to spray,
And cheer'd the forest with his artless lay,
Or fluttered o'er the purling brook at will,
Sung in the dale or soar'd above the hill.
Such are the liberal charms of college life,
Where pleasure flows without a breeze of strife;
And such would be my pain if cast away,
Without the blooms of study to display.
Beware, ye college birds, again beware,
And shun the fowler with his subtile snare;
Nor fall as one from Eden, stript of all
The life and beauty of your native hall;
Nor from the garden of your honor go,
Whence all the streams of fame and wisdom flow;
Where brooding Milton's theme purls sweet along

With Pope upon the gales of epic song;
Where you may trace a bland Demosthenes,
Whose oratoric pen ne'er fails to please;
And Plato, with immortal Cicero,
And with the eloquence of Horace glow;
There cull the dainties of a great Ainsworth,
Who sets the feast of ancient language forth;
Or glide with Ovid on his simple stream,
And catch the heat from Virgil's rural beam;
Through Addison you trace creation's fire,
And all the rapid wheels of time admire;
Or pry with Paley's theologic rays,
And hail the hand of wisdom as you gaze;
 Up Murray's pleasant hill you strive to climb,
To gain a golden summit all sublime,
And plod through conic sections all severe,
Which to procure is pleasure true and dear.
The students' pensive mind is often stung,
Whilst blundering through the Greek and Latin tongue;
Parsing in grammars which may suit the whole,
And will the dialect of each control.
Now let us take a retrospective view,
And whilst we pause, observe a branch or two.
 Geography and Botany unfold
Their famous charms like precious seeds of gold;
Zoology doth all her groups descry,
And with Astronomy we soar on high;
But pen and ink and paper all would fail,
To write one third of this capacious tale.
Geography presents her flowery train,
Describes the mountain and surveys the plain,
Measures the sounding rivers as they grow,
Unto the trackless deeps to which they flow:
She measures well her agriculture's stores,
Which meet her commerce on the golden shore,
Includes the different seasons of the year,
And changes which pervade the atmosphere,
Treats of the dread phenomena which rise
In different shapes on earth, or issue from the skies;
She points in truth to Lapland's frozen clime,
And nicely measures all the steps of time;
Unfolds the vast equator's burning line,
Where all the stores of heat dissolve and shine;
Describes the earth as unperceived she rolls,
Her well–poised axis placed upon the poles.

Botany, whose charms her florists well display,
Whose lavish odours swell the pomp of May,
Whose curling wreaths the steady box adorn,
And fill with fragrance all the breeze of morn.
Through various means her plants are oft applied,
Improved by art, and well by nature tried;
Thro' her, the stores of herbage are unroll'd,
All which compose the vegetable world;
Even the sensitives, which feel and shrink,
From slightest touches, though they cannot think,
Not yet rejoice, void of the power to fear,
Or sense to smell, to see, to taste, or hear.
Zoology, with her delightful strain,
Doth well the different animals explain;
From multipedes to emmets in the dust,
And all the groveling reptiles of disgust;
She well descries the filthy beetle blind,
With insects high and low of every kind;
She with her microscope surveys the mite,
Which ne'er could be beheld by naked sight;
Thence she descends into the boundless deep,
Where dolphins play and monsters slowly creep;
Explores the foaming main from shore to shore,
And hears with awe the dshing sea bull roar;
Traces enormous whales exploding high
Their floods of briny water to the sky;
Desribes the quadrupeds of ever shape,
The bear, the camel, elephant and ape,
And artful monkey, which but lack to talk,
And like the human kind uprightly walk.
Astronomy, with her aerial powers,
Lifts us above this dreary globe of ours;
Throughout the realms of ether's vast expanse,
Her burning wings our towering minds advance;
Measures her tropic well from line to line,
And marks her rolling planets as they shine;
Describes the magnitude of every star,
And thence pursues her comets as they roll afar.
But nature never yet was half explored,
Though by philosopher and bard adored;
Astronomer and naturalist expire,
And languish that they could ascend no higher;
Expositors of words in every tongue,
Writers of prose and scribblers of song,
Would fail with all their mathematic powers,

And vainly study out their fleeting hours.
Sir Walter Raleigh, Pen and Roberson,
With Morse and Snowden, who are dead and gone,
They all were, though mused their lives away,
And left ten thousand wonders to display.
And though the fiery chemists probe the mine
The subterraneous bodies to define;
Though melting flames the force of matter try,
Rocks mix'd with brass and gold to pieces fly;
And those who follow the electric muse,
Amidst the wilds of vast creation loose
Themselves like pebbles in the swelling main,
And strive for naught these wanders to explain;
Galvin himself, the monarch of the whole,
Would blush his empty parchments to unroll.
These different branches to one ocean go,
Where all the streams of life together flow,
Where perfect wisdom swells the tide of joy,
A tide which must eternity employ;
A boundless sea of love without a shore,
Whose pleasure ebbs and flows forever more;
Volume Divine! O thou the sacred dew,
Thy fadeless fields see elders passing through,
Thy constant basis must support the whole,
The cabinet and alcove of the soul;
It matters not through what we may have pass'd,
To thee for sure support we fly at last;
Encyclopedias we may wander o'er,
And study every scientific lore,
Ancient and modern authors we may read,
The soul must starve or on thy pastures feed.
These bibliothic charms would surely fall,
And life grow dim within this college wall,
The wheels of study in the mind would tire,
If not supported by thy constant fire;
Greatest of all the precepts ever taught
Maps and vocabularies dearly bought,
Burns with his harp, Scott, Cambell, and their flowers,
Will shrink without the everlasting showers;
Theology, thou sweetest science yet,
Beneath whose boughs the silent classics sit,
And thus imbibe the sacred rays divine,
Which make the mitred faculty to shine;
O for a gleam of Buck, immortal muse,
With elder Scott and Henry to peruse;

These lines which did a secret bliss inspire,
And set the heads, the hearts, the tongues, on fire.
Such is the useful graduate indeed,
Not merely at the bar in law to plead,
Nor a physician best to heal the flesh,
But all the mystic power of soul and flesh;
On such a senior let archangels smile,
And all the students imitate his style,
Who bears with joy the mission all divine,
The beams of sanctitude, a Paul benign;
Whose sacred call is to evangelise,
A gospel prince, a legate of the skies,
Whose bright diploma is a deed from heaven,
The palm of love, the wreath of sins forgiven.

THE GRADUATE LEAVING COLLEGE.

What summons do I hear?
The morning peal, departure's knell;
My eyes let fall a friendly tear,
And bid this place farewell.

Attending servants come,
The carriage wheels like thunders roar,
To bear the pensive seniors home,
Here to be seen no more.

Pass one more transient night,
The morning sweeps the college clean;
The graduate takes his last long flight,
No more in college seen.

The bee, which courts the flower,
Must with some pain itself employ,
And then fly, at the day's last hour,
Home to its hive with joy.

TO THE KING OF MACEDONIA.

Phillip, thou art mortal!

Thou may'st with pleasure hail the dawn,
And greet the morning's eye;
Remember, king, the night comes on,
The fleeting day will soon be gone,
Not distant, loud proclaims the funeral tone,
Phillip, thou hast to die.

With thee thy dame, the queen of birds,
May spread her wing to fly;
Or smile to trace the numerous herds,
Thunders from the Lord of lords,
I hear some peal surpassing human words,
Philip, thou hast to die.

Thou mayst thy mighty host survey
And neighboring kings defy,
Whilst round thy retinues flit gay,
Beneath thy pomp's imperial ray,
Make merry on the tide of joy to day,
To—morrow thou shalt die.

I heave to hear the day's last peal,
A sorrow teeming sigh;
The morning's flutt'ring bird has flown,
The roses fade, so quickly blown,
The lofty king falls robeless from his throne,
Philip was born to die.

'Twas thus the haughty king of France
Strove to ascend on high;
Lifting his adamantine lance,
He bade his dauntless war—horse prance,
Defied the world, and rode the car of chance,
To rage, to fume and die.

Thus vile, thus obstinately vain,
He pours his distant brag,
Regardless of his millions slain,
Regales his pale surviving train,
Was but wraped in his infernal chain,
Dies on the ocean crag.

This faithful lesson read to all
Creation, far and nigh,
It is the fate, from Adam's fall,
The swain, the king, the low, and tall,
The watchman of the grave must give the call,
Mortal, thou hast to die.

DIVISION OF AN ESTATE.

It well bespeaks a man beheaded, quite
Divested of the laurel robe of life,
When every member struggles for its base,
The head; the power of order now recedes,
Unheeded efforts rise on every side,
With dull emotion rolling through the brain
Of apprehending slaves. The flocks and herds,
In sad confusion, now run to and fro,
And seem to ask, distressed, the reason why
That they are thus prostrated. Howl, ye dogs!
Ye cattle, low! ye sheep, astonish'd, bleat!
Ye bristling swine, trudge squealing through the glades,
Void of an owner to impart your food!
Sad horses, lift your heads and neigh aloud,
And caper frantic from the dismal scene;
Mow the last food upon your grass—clad lea,
And leave a solitary home behind,
In hopeless widowhood no longer gay!
The trav'ling sun of gain his journey ends
In unavailing pain; he sets with tears;
A king sequester'd sinking from his throne,
Succeeded by a train of busy friends,
Like stars which rise with smiles, to mark the flight

Of awful Phoebus to another world;
Stars after stars in fleet succession rise
Into the wide empire of fortune clear,
Regardless of the donor of their lamps,
Like heirs forgetful of parental care,
Without a grateful smile or filial tear,
Redound in rev'rence to expiring age.
But soon parental benediction flies
Like vivid meteors; in a moment gone,
As though they ne'er had been. But O! the state,
The dark suspense in which poor vassals stand,
Each mind upon the spire of chance hangs fluctuant;
The day of separation is at hand;
Imagination lifts her gloomy curtains,
Like ev'ning's mantle at the flight of day,
Thro' which the trembling pinnacle we spy,
On which we soon must stand with hopeful smiles,
Or apprehending frowns; to tumble on
The right or left forever.

PRIDE IN HEAVEN.

On heaven's ethereal plain,
With hostile rage ambition first begun,
When the arch rebel strove himself to reign
And take Jehovah's throne.
Swift to the fight the seraphim
On floods of pride were seen to swim,
And bold defy the power supreme,
And thus their God disown.

High on a dome of state,
From azure fields he cast his daring eye,
Licentious trains his magazines await,
At whose command they fly.
The gloom excludes celestial charms,
When all the angels rush to arms,
Heaven shakes beneath the vast alarms,
And earth begins to sigh.

Eternal mountains move,
And seven—fold thunders rock the hills below,
While starry throngs desert the worlds above,
Beneath Jehovah's brow.
O Lucifer, thou morning son,
To glut thy pide what hast thou done?
Sing, O ye heavens, the plague is gone,
And weep, thou earth, for wo.

Creation felt the fall,
And trembling nature heav'd a dismal groan;
For that rebellion brought her into thrall,
She must her fate bemoan;
See angels fall no more to rise,
And feed the worm that never dies;
No ear of grace can hear their cries,
And hoarse lamenting tone.

Weak nature lay exposed,
And felt the wound in pleasing hate conceal'd;
And, void of fear, the secret charm disclosed
Which ev'ry ill reveal'd.
The venom struck through ev'ry vein,
And every creature felt the pain;
But undefiled a lamb was slain,
By which the wound was heal'd.

TO MISS TEMPE.

Bless'd hope, when Tempe takes her last long flight,
And leaves her lass—lorn lover to complain,
Like Luna mantling o'er the brow of night,
Thy glowing wing dispels the gloom of pain.

Yes, wondrous hope, when Tempe sails afar,
Thy vital lamp remains to burn behind,
While by—gone pleasure, like a setting star,
Rejects her glory o'er the twilight mind.

Thy glowing wing was never spread to tire,
Expanded o'er the mansion of the brave,
To fan and set the heaving breast on fire,
That soars in triumph from affliction's wave.

Then, Tempe, dart along the ocean drear,
Hope yet forbids my cheerful soul to weep,
But marks thy passage with affection's tear,
And hails thee on the bosom of the deep.

Farewell, since thou wilt leave thy native shore,
I smile to think I am not left alone;
Auspicious hope shall yet my peace restore,
When thou art from the beach forever gone.

MAN A TORCH.

Blown up with painful care, and hard to light,
A glimmering torch, blown in a moment out;
Suspended by a webb, an angler's bait,
Floating at stake along the stream of chance,
Snatch'd from its hook by the fish of poverty.
A silent cavern is his last abode;
The king's repository, veil'd with gloom,
The umbrage of a thousand oziers; bowed,
The couch of hallowed bones, the slave's asylum,
The brave's retreat, and end of ev'ry care.

CPSIA information can be obtained
at www.ICGtesting.com
Printed in the USA
BVHW05005506012122
625206BV00007B/716

9 781162 705040